Big Machines

Big Machines Rescue!

Catherine Veitch

Raintree

Raintree is an imprint of Capstone Global Library Limited, a company incorporated in England and Wales having its registered office at 7 Pilgrim Street, London, EC4V 6LB – Registered company number: 6695582

www.raintreepublishers.co.uk
myorders@raintreepublishers.co.uk

Text © Capstone Global Library Limited 2015
The moral rights of the proprietor have been asserted.

Edited by Helen Cox Cannons and Kathryn Clay
Designed by Tim Bond and Peggie Carley
Picture research by Mica Brancic and Tracy Cummins
Production by Helen McCreath
Originated by Capstone Global Library Ltd
Printed and bound in China by Leo Paper Group

ISBN 978 1 406 28458 4
18 17 16 15 14
10 9 8 7 6 5 4 3 2 1

British Library Cataloguing in Publication Data
A full catalogue record for this book is available from the British Library.

Acknowledgements
We would like to thank the following for permission to reproduce photographs:

Alamy: © Dave.J.Smith/Naude, 14, 15, © david tipling, 10, 11, © Ian Patrick, 16, 17, ©imagebroker/Wolfgang Bechtold, 4, 5, © johnrochaphoto, 18, 19, 22b; Getty Images: AFP PHOTO / JIJI PRESS, 20, 21, E+/Rich Yasick, front cover; iStock: © Nasowas, 8, 9, 22a, back cover; NASA: 6, 7, 22d, back cover; Newscom: courtesy of Boston Dynamics, 21; Shutterstock: Jerry Sharp, 12, 13, 22c.

Every effort has been made to contact copyright holders of material reproduced in this book. Any omissions will be rectified in subsequent printings if notice is given to the publisher.

All the Internet addresses (URLs) given in this book were valid at the time of going to press. However, due to the dynamic nature of the Internet, some addresses may have changed, or sites may have changed or ceased to exist since publication. While the author and publisher regret any inconvenience this may cause readers, no responsibility for any such changes can be accepted by either the author or the publisher.

Contents

Some words are shown in bold, **like this.** You can find out what they mean by looking in the glossary.

Ice breaker

Super

Big

Mighty

Size

submersible

Divers reach the submarine in a **submersible**. They collect the crew and bring them back to safety.

Airport crash tender

Special fire engines are made just for airports. They are called airport crash tenders.

monitor

Super
Big Mighty
Size

A hose called a **monitor** sits on top of the vehicle. The hose sprays foam over a fire to put out the flames.

Search and rescue helicopter

Super
Big Mighty
Size

A search and rescue helicopter carries plenty of **fuel** for faraway rescues. It can stay in the air for two to three hours.

winch

A **winch** lifts injured people up into the helicopter.

ladder truck

A ladder truck is a fire engine with a long ladder. Firefighters use the ladder to rescue people from tall buildings.

Super

Big Mighty

Size

The longest ladder on a fire engine is about 30 metres (98 feet) long. That's about as tall as six adult giraffes standing on top of each other!

Tow truck

A tow truck rescues vehicles that have broken down or been in crashes.

boom

Tow trucks use a hook attached to a **boom** to haul vehicles.

14

Lifeboat

A lifeboat helps in an **emergency**. It rescues people from boats or from the water. Then the people are taken back to shore.

Lifeboats

Snow ambulance

Two large tracks help this snow ambulance move easily over the snow.

The blade at the back clears a path in the snow.

tracks

Super

Big

Mighty

Size

Kässbohrer

blade

19

Sizing things up: rescue robots

T-53 Enryu

Height..........2.7 metres (9 feet)
Weight.........4.5 metric tons (5 tons)
Special skills ....Can lift 200 kilograms
(440 pounds)

Big Dog

Height	0.76 metres (2.5 feet)
Weight	109 kilograms (240 pounds)
Special skills	Can lift 154 kilograms (340 pounds)
	Can travel 32 kilometres (20 miles) in one day

Quiz

How much of a Machine Mega-Brain are you?
Can you match each machine name to its correct photo?

**snow ambulance • submarine rescue ship
airport crash tender • ladder truck**

Check the answers on the opposite page
to see if you got all four correct.

Glossary

boom a metal arm

emergency an unexpected, dangerous event

fuel a substance that gives power to machines

monitor a special hose on an airport fire engine

submarine a ship that can travel underwater

submersible a small craft that works underwater

winch equipment used for lifting or pulling something heavy

Quiz answers:
1. airport crash tender 2. snow ambulance
3. ladder truck 4. submarine rescue ship

23

Find out more

Books

Emergency Vehicles (How it Works), Steve Parker (Miles Kelly Publishing Ltd, 2010)

Sea Rescue (Emergency Vehicles), Deborah Chancellor (Franklin Watts, 2012)

Websites

www.juniorcitizen.org.uk/kids

rnli.org/shorething/Pages/default.aspx

Index